Said the Swing to the Hoop

D. Colin

Printed in the United States of America
First Printing, 2019

ISBN 0-9000000-0-0

Empress Bohemia Books

www.dcolin.com

"And I am all the things I have ever loved..."
Toni Morrison

Said the Swing to the Hoop

I think we might be the best
parts of the playground. We make hearts
fly a little. See the sky different. You see
it's all about perspective. We know what it's like
to have legs push for us
on a swing, to a rim. We know about trash
talk. Kids seeing who can go higher. We
know about late nights & street lights.
We know about emotions
when they go wrong. See,
no one goes to the slide
when they're sad. We got swag.
We be a new way to see clouds
before they rain. We just might be the best
parts of the playground. We see dreams big
as life. The ground on one side. The sky on the other.
Only difference, they have to jump
through hoops to get yours/swing a lot to get mine.
We see sweat & pain & tears & scrapes—we see
blood. Sometimes
it's not the kind from victory—
that kind of play. Ground up. Like I lost
my memory. Like I forgot the way laughter sounded
on the way down. I just want to keep them lifted
off the ground. Too many of them are laying
on the ground. I just can't swing
that kind of pain. Tell me how do you
keep them above the rim? Maybe I can
keep them reaching for the sky.
Real talk. We be the best parts of the playground.
We be the only ones have them reaching
for something bigger than themselves.

Nineteen Ninety-Seven

Year of the Spice Girl & Sojourner on Mars,
I rocked to a heavy bass called Hip Hop
while Beethoven streamed through my fingers
on a piano. I listened to the sound of
my voice in song only when I taught
kids in my church to sing & when Total let out
the hardest *can't you see* from my television.

Secretly, I wanted to be a star,
wrote rap lyrics to the Man called Method,
dropped bars on a playground
to my friends & we called ourselves
the Basis Crew—
      Black
      Attractive
      Sistahs
      in
      Style.
That year we worked music & basketball
into our legs—danced in the talent show
to Quad City DJ's Space Jam. I learned
to butterfly & had to borrow
my father's jeans because I didn't own
my own & how—I wondered,
would the preacher's daughter
win a grammy
wearing only skirts. Then Missy let me know
the meaning of supa dupa fly,
rockin' a garbage bag.

Nineteen Ninety-Seven—an ear on
a Holyfield got bit off by Tyson
OJ, not the juice, was found not guilty
& Juicy blared from every speaker in a radius
of Brooklyn cause Biggie got shot & for real,
I wished it was all a dream.

A kid about my age
set his apartment on fire & his grandmother
died. Her name was Betty Shabazz. I watched
a re-airing of the royal wedding after
Princess Diana died in a car crash & I cried
—even revolution & fairy tales
could get the business of death.

Nineteen Ninety-Seven—
UCONN ended their season 33-1
losing to Tennessee in the Regional Final.
I rooted for the Knicks with all my life,
flicked my wrist like I was John Starks,
backed up in the paint like I was Patrick Ewing,
believed I'd be the first woman in the NBA
until nineteen ninety-seven when I changed
the dream to New York Liberty & I practiced hard,
made plans to play ball for Geno Auriemma,
drew two hands on the wall of my basement to
practice passing the ball to no body & played,
no contacts, no goggles & our team sucked. I remember
a game—whatever points to zero & we
were the zero. I drew a foul
no time on the clock,

whole team rooting for me to score
the only   points   of   the   game
from the foul line, a hoop in my clouded vision—
end score was whatever points
to zero. It's appropriate then
that Daria aired for the first time that year,
I fell in love with Tiger Woods only to realize
golf too rich for my blood & I was still rockin' to
I can't stand the rain, 'gainst my window
but kept playing the piano—Tchaikovsky's Swan Lake

To this day Love & Basketball
& the question:
when did you fall in love with Hip Hop?
tie a neat knot in my throat
because of nineteen ninety-seven,
the year dreams died
quiet like shadows disappearing in the shade.

My PK Checklist (1983-2001)

✔ Tell the entire kindergarten class there is no Santa
✔ Accept Jesus as your personal savior (age seven)
✔ Get baptized (age fourteen)

✔ Start teaching Sunday School (at the age of twelve.
   Do this for twelve years)
✔ Direct the children's choir—subsequently
   the young adult choir
✔ Don't wear shorts or pants (with the exception of
   sports, the school talent show & the one time your
   cousin talks you into daisy dukes for which you will
   suffer dire consequences—

☐ Listen only to Gospel music

✔ Don't pierce your ears (You'll wait twenty-seven
years
   just for the courage.)
✔ Don't wear makeup (except foundation—
   foundation is okay)
✔ Don't go to the movies (but then there was that
   first time   my best friend & I
   got caught—having gone with dates.)

☐ Don't drink alcohol (with the exception of kremas)

✔Don't rock any fake hair (negotiations allowed
   only when I am part of a bridal party)

☐ Testify

✔Only wear one piece bathing suits (especially
   the kind with the little skirt at the bottom

☐ Don't go to prom (or lie about going.)

✔Plan the youth revival
✔Be a role model
✔Let go of frivolous dreams such as ballet or
  figure skating or gymnastics. (You know you can't
wear
  the costumes.)
✔Eventually quit all teams that practice and/or compete
  on weekends i.e. basketball or track & field or
  step, etc. etc.

☐ Write poems only for the church

✔Direct Sunday night service
✔Sing in the adult choir

☐ Play piano in the church

✔Choreograph for the praise dancers (It's the closest
  you'll ever get to ballet.)
✔Be an usher

☐ Be a role model (as in make no mistakes—ever.)

☐ Marry a man to follow in Pastor's footsteps

☐ Stay

☐ No pressure

☐ No pressure

☐ No pressure

Soutien

When I was eight, I played house with my cousins,
all braids & bright-eyed, the only girl in the room.
I don't remember why but I started to change
my clothes. There I was—bare—flat chest—shirtless
when my mom walked in the room & before I
could say a thing, I was on my knees—
shirt demanded back on my body
snot faced & kneeling until papi came home.
I learned my first gendered lesson that day:
that boys could bare their chests & girls could not
that I couldn't play a boy if I was ever
playing house again.

When I was ten, I got my period for the first time
I thought death had found me & my mother
told me to stay away from boys
When I was eleven, my mother took me shopping
for my first soutien. In French it literally means support.
I only ever knew it to mean bra in Kreyol.
One of the girls in my class already had melons
Mine were more like grapes—thought maybe
that's why they're called training bras...
They train grapes   to be melons?

When I was sixteen, I was still waiting
didn't know how many cups larger
just knew mine were less than
half full than my mother's.
We shared food, sometimes a skirt
we could share a laugh
but we'd never share a bra.
My itty-bitties had only ever learned to be peaches
& I was told to cover all the way to the top
so I hushed my peaches up under loose plaid shirts

lest the loudness of their sweet attract flies.

I used to think about the women in Haiti, bare
breasts & bathing—shifting freely
beneath a shirt. How mine weren't large
enough to worry for/that I had been more
Colin than Danielle. A boy protecting myself from boys
how a soutien never supported me that way
how it's only function was to cover them up twice
how it only ever stopped them from dancing.

I've been training them
to restrain themselves
to talk less
to not show up or show off
when I've only ever wanted them to be free
like that little girl
all braids & bright-eyed
being anything she wanted
even if it was a boy
instead of protecting herself
from them all.

Building a Bear

There's a memory I have walking
up Locust Hill or a street in Spring Valley somewhere...
Cold air chips at my skin. I reach for someone—
my mother—my uncle—my cousin—to
pick me up   but no one does.

There I am, snot chiseled
a few degrees below my nose,
water frozen on my cheeks,
They all say I am *too heavy* &
I think maybe it was a dream

except all have told me this story
that I was a *ti boul*—a little ball
in other words a butterball—which sounds
much more adorable than what it
actually is—a ball   of butter.

I've been told how the doctor
placed me on a special diet,
how I'd cry for food, how my mom
would cave into my cravings,
because what's a West Indian mother to do
other than feed her child?

In fifth grade, someone called me
fat & I collected teddy bears until
senior year of high school—maybe
it was how they had round

bellies & everyone loves them any-
how, holds their squish
willfully in their hands.

I ate peanut butter & jelly every
day for three years & I mean I
love peanut butter & jelly but
I punished my fat self &
first time I thought of suicide,
I chose the   slowest   way   possible

Just don't eat

Just don't eat anything at all.

When someone remembers the child of me
says some kind words
as a compliment to my size
how they never thought I'd turn
out with *this* body,
sometimes
I remember my teddy bear
belly & how I'm still learning
to hold myself close.

Broke just like that
after Patrick Rosal

Nina sings *the rock cried out, I ain't gonna hide you*
& alone in my room I search for the rock
so we can talk about protection
because on that day
I realized, the rock might not be
on my side, that I haven't learned to run
from sinnermen, that I think, their sins contagious
common like cold like aching fingers
lost their dance, like tongues
on ice holding on
two languages instead of three
& I wonder if that makes the trinity
less holy, to be a sliver of moon
light sonata, heavy on keys that no
longer open doors or see sharp & just like
that I need glasses for everything but my eyes
to know my body & where it hurts
like how my mouth don't fit round that no more
like how I be flat on my back painting notes on ceilings
with my eyes shut & throat raspy
in search of the right pitch for no
but all I can hiss in a prayer is
what's the matter with you rock

Don't   you   know   that   I   need   you?

& now, I am a metronome wandering for a song,
like a river lost at sea I am bleeding
there is no more staccato. Just like that—

it occurs to me why I quit piano
why I am listening to one
waning echo of a pedal & my foot
left here
      tapping
           nothing

                but the

                      floor.

Broken-winged

Hold fast to dreams
for if dreams die
life is a broken-winged bird
that cannot fly.

Langston Hughes

Today, I was told I'm fly.
Two feet on the ground,
sleep in my eyes,
teardrop wrapped
around my heart,
word like honey dripping
tasteless today.
Fly supposed to sound
like wings kissed the air
but this blows. How do I
hold fast to dreams

like birds crashed
into high rise windows?
Never saw the glass
coming. No directions
exist for mourning
anyone but a child
in particular, dead
in the body or in the ground
reserves a strange howl
for if dreams die.

I remember the day a bird
flew directly for my face,
circled back again & again
my only protection

a book in my hands
Today, there are three
crows settled on the snow.
I freeze by the door,
whisper hello but
life is a broken-winged bird

hobbling, eyes wide open &
I still fear them all.
A friend told me once,
that crows emerge to
echo voices of the dead.
Maybe I should listen to signs,
that ancestors, especially
children lost, find wings
borrow them for a while
to save the parts of them
that cannot fly

fly

fly

fly

fly

fly

fly

Stay Alive

I met my boyfriend at the candy shop

Actually his place, 1999, a Thursday & the heat that day
had nothing to do with us. Actually he was into my best
friend. Actually she was into his cousin. Actually we were
there for them.
I, a second choice—a last resort—a default.

He bought me ice cream. He bought me cake.

Actually, he never bought me a thing. Actually, I never
wanted him to.

He brought me home with a belly ache.

Actually I brought him home & no one ever told me I'd
learn to claw flesh & I could not understand why
I had painted the walls pink. My favorite color
had always been blue.

Mama, Mama, I feel sick.

Actually, I kept it secret—for a long time—but yes—
yes, I felt sick. Actually, it looked like my head down
during American history—fifth period,
the smooth top of my desk, wet & chemistry—failing
chemistry & gasping
just above the surface of an F
in AP English. I became sculptor of my cheeks
when the music died & trapped,
I ran to escape my body.

Call the doctor! Quick, quick, quick!

Actually, there was no phone call/no rape kit/no police
report & nothing quick about it. Nothing quick about
no nothing at all.

Doctor, doctor will I die?

Actually, I asked God. Because
I stayed. Because what else did I have
to offer anyone, he hadn't already
taken from me. Because even when I left,
he came back & the last time,
night before Christmas Eve. My body——
pajamas—slippers—headscarf— a tee.
My voice—a scream/a whisper.
Muscle tight around my throat.
Scrape of concrete stairs on this dead end street.
I'll kill you he said. *Dead on the street* he said
so I went, cold air swallowing me whole.

Count to five and stay alive.

I counted my fingers to feel them.
Counted the cars whizzing by.
Counted seconds/minutes/hours.
Inhabited repetition
stay alive
stay alive
stay alive

(there is no room in a poem
for my survival)

One—

This time, I called cops.
There is a report somewhere
a file, an old restraining order.
I never saw him again.
But I hold my keys tight

when I walk home alone.

Two—

I left my hometown. I am sorry.
It was Park Ave. The route home. It was
the front steps he choked me on.
the intersection I tried
to wave a car down for
help. my story in the paper—Woman kidnapped...
It was the ghost of him
everywhere.

Three—

he was replaced by another.
I stopped taking cold medicine
with drowsiness as a side affect.

Four—

he was replaced by another.
I moved twice in three months
so that one wouldn't know my address.
I cut my hair. I cut them all out.

Five—

I held my name
in my hands & it became a poem.
I replaced them all
with myself. Cracked open.
the mess of my yolk
fried in the sun
a new thing.

I'm alive!

I am.
I am.
I am.

I cry for little Black girls

I cry for little Black girls on street corners
whose fathers don't know them
whose mothers don't care for them.
Little Black girls
playing hopscotch & singing,
double-dutch & chanting

Down

    down baby,

        down by the rollercoaster,

        sweet, sweet baby

        I'll never

        let you

        go

Shimmy shimmy coco
        POP

            shimmy shimmy
            POW

Shimmy shimmy coco
        PUFF

            shimmy shimmy
            POW

I cry for little Black girls who don't know
how to make a dollar out of fifteen cents
or how to make sense out of no options
when no dollars are left. I cry
for the thoughts that will creep
into their heads about the standards of beauty,

for little Black girls searching for the bluest eye
or haven't learned there are more
beautiful things than Beyonce
girls who commit suicide when the rainbow is enuf
because their dreams dried up like a raisin in the sun
all while their eyes were watching God

So now let's get the rhythm of the head
                    DING DONG
                              [move head from side to side]
Let's get the rhythm of the head
                    DING DONG
                              [move head from side to side]

I cry for little Black girls stripped
of their mind like slavery times
Use the body. Take the mind.
Touch her body. Take her mind.
Rape her body. Take her mind.
Girls who sing
I wish I had a nickel
I wish I had a dime
I wish I had a boyfriend
who would kiss me all the time

& then she gets no nickel
she doesn't get a dime
instead she gets a boyfriend
who beats her all the time
instead she gets a boyfriend
in prison doing time

instead she gets a boyfriend
who will never have the time
& she will stay because
she doesn't know, she is worth the time.
What's left is a body. What's gone is her mind.

Now let's get the rhythm of the hands

CLAP CLAP

[strike palms together to make thunder]
Let's get the rhythm of the hands

CLAP CLAP

[strike palms together to make thunder]

I cry for little Black girls who will never write
tree poems because there are no trees outside
just concrete & like Nikki Giovanni,
they'll realize these are not poetic times at all.
I cry for little Black girls laying on the asphalt
who don't know it's not their fault
red lines break their neighborhoods like fault lines
that trees might not be the only thing
not growing & society will deem lattes
more important than a school
that cares their notebooks be scribbled with
dreams America won't read.

So now let' get the rhythm of the feet

STOMP STOMP

[intentionally step foot to the earth to quake]
Let's get the rhythm of the feet

STOMP STOMP

[intentionally step foot to the earth to quake]

Let's get the rhythm of the hot dog
                    [POWER POSE. Move body in a loop
                    like an invisible hoolahoop]
Let's get the rhythm of the hot dog
                    [POWER POSE. Move body in a
                    loop like an invisible hoolahoop]

I cry for little Black girls who have no one
to feed their stomachs, no one to feed their minds
for the nights they will have no place to go
for the tears they will shed & for the ones ahead of them
who won't look back to carry them
out of the pits they fall in.
I cry for their tired feet & hunger to be free
I cry for little Black girls who haven't lived enough life
to understand what I mean
but will grow up & see
& when they do
                    when they do

I hope I'm not alone singing

Down down baby
            GET OFF of the rollercoaster
                        Sweet Sweet baby
I'll   never let   you   go

                                    TAKE BACK

the rhythm of your head

                                    TAKE BACK

the rhythm of your hands

the rhythm of your feet

the rhythm of your whole

being.

TAKE BACK

TAKE BACK

Exit Stage Left

Scene One—We have been over this already.

Scene Two through Six—same lines different actor
Stories are supposed to progress not repeat
but we knew you could handle trauma again.
Please be off book by next rehearsal.

We know opening act broke your leg & you've been
walking with a limp ever since
so we put in a long intermission—
too much pressure riding on the hopes of Act II.
The show must go on. The show must go on—
no matter what.

Are you still with us?

Larger than Life

Mrs. Large was a tall woman, broad shoulders
a walk that could wake a room. I was eleven.
Little. Shy. Full of quiet. Nothing of boom.

Sixth graders were afraid to make it
to 8th grade because she was everything of
boom. Voice & blackboard & chalk.

She knew how to write & erase fear in a child.
Mrs. Large was large,
silenced a class just by looking & waiting.

She chilled in her power, cool as shaved ice
on a summer day. Cool as the gray on her
head. She danced in her passion.

First teacher I ever met who loved what she did.
I was eleven. Mrs. Large asked my
6th grade teacher for the top of the class.

That was me. The nerd. The bored kid.
She asked if I would like to write a
speech for the school contest, then speak

it OUT LOUD. Me.
Little. Shy. Full of quiet. No.
Mrs. Large didn't take no for an answer.

She heard possibility. She heard nothing of no
& everything of boom. Maybe
once upon a time she was shy too.

She was after school & pen & paper &
grammar. She was hope & ambition & challenge.

First time I ever spoke in front of the school,

I thought I would die, faint to no waking.
Mrs. Large said she was my audience.
She was large enough to fill

the whole room. She was the only one there.
She was stage & mic & front row.
I never told her. I hope that she knows.

I am writer because of her. I am stage & mic &
poet & might. I am light on
words because of her,

the teacher who set the precedent.
told me once, I could be the first black woman
president & I believed her.

She gave me more than gerunds & definitions,
more than verbs & sentence structure.
Most students had her for one year; I had her

for three, working on speeches,
working on me.
Mrs. Large was larger than life to me

until I was larger than life to myself.

Toussaint

In middle school, I remember reading
Toussaint L'Ouverture's biography [not at school
but from my father's library] & so what it was
in French; didn't matter that I didn't understand it
all, long as I understood revolution & freedom & Haiti
& Black & somehow I was all of those things
even if at that age, when I put bobos & barrettes to
rest & listened more intently to the blood
between my legs, I was unsure if I'd revolved
around anything or if I was free at all
but I knew Ayiti poured through me like a libation &
I was Black like an eraser slowly
clapping out chalk & Toussaint
wasn't just in this book—It was the last name
of my first crush—Black like me—Haitian
like me & I remember the gap
in his teeth when he smiled—how he was
the darkest boy in my class—how I was
the darkest girl in my class. Felt like we made
part of the same mud/wanted to shape us into
something beautiful & of course he
should have liked me back—all Black girl
kinky curl and sos pwa. I was supposed to
taste like home so of course he was supposed to
like me back until 6th grade when Carla
I think was her name, carried a woman
twice her age in her chest—how the nuns
had to always remind her to button
up her shirt—how the boys
drooled & 7th grade when the goddess Athena
came to our school wrapped in butterscotch
with Brooklyn on her breath & hair that blew
in the wind & I never did like me
until we sat next to each other in 8th grade

& he could see all my answers.
Poor boy didn't know that even if
he didn't love me, he loved my mind
& it was the first time in all those years
I realized without the words to articulate it just right
that maybe, I didn't like him at all—that maybe
I just wanted a part of Toussaint
I could call my own—that really I was looking for
my own reflection & all the while
She was who I loved when the boys
didn't come home
She was who I loved all along.

miracle

mir·a·cle | \ ˈmir-i-kəl \

Definition of *miracle*

verb

1: ~~an extraordinary event~~ manifesting divine intervention
in human affairs

//She miracles her way through this life.

noun

2: an extremely outstanding or unusual ~~event, thing, or~~
accomplishment

// It's a miracle she made it this far.

adjective

3: ~~Christian Science:~~ a **divine**~~ly natural phenomenon~~
~~experienced humanly as the fulfillment of spiritual la~~

//A miracle baby, after all, is one fighting before
ever tasting air.

A waft of flame on melting wax

to my maternal grandmother

I imagine your fingers round & calloused
folded together, a conjured
prophecy on your thin lips:

"On the seventh day of March,
I will be buried. She will be born &
she shall be called ti miracle."

Been told I have your eyes.
In another life, I must have been
broken over sugarcane.

Next time it is the seventh of March
I will light a multitude of candles
whisper happy birthday to us all.

A dead black bird lay at my feet this morning
Is this your heart holding many a secret song
your blood boiled like sos pwa black & thick over rice?

As sound under water I hear
you say mwen manke ou
& who am I, if not reincarnation,

birth & death drinking from the same gourd?
Our name must be gwo miracle,
only wicks & days of melting wax between us.

The girl dream

& the girl, called into a room—three boys & a girl—the
girl, the only girl—& my grandpa asked what they
wanted to be—& the girl bright-eyed chest out back
straight clear voice said—lawyer—the girl made of river
bed and dirt road—fried plantain and piklis—coal fire &
cast iron pot—said—lawyer—not two weeks later my
grandpa pulled the girl out of school—sent her to learn
how to sew & cook—the girl supposed to be a boy's
dream—not dream like one—not supposed to be lawyer—
or bold—or big— or speak loud—or speak—the girl
skipped sewing class—used pocket change from Gran Tiso
to buy fresco & watch people walk on Champ de Mars
without anyone knowing—the girl a protest—the girl still
dreaming in view of the presidential palace

The girl becomes a woman—becomes a wife—becomes my
mother—my mother carries three girls & a boy— like the
tethered—like a reckoning—I am the only child to survive
the terrain of her womb—the only girl—the only dream
left

My mother immigrant. My mother night school &
wrestling Kreyol on her tongue. My mother lover of
coconut flesh & peanut brittle. My mother loud. My
mother sacrifice. My mother first lady of the church. My
mother housekeeper for a living. My mother
mathematician— making a dollar out of un goud—less
than fifteen cents—& one day she taught me a lesson in a
white woman's bathroom—pointed to the toilet she just
cleaned—said this job—in particular & overall—is not for

you—said you could be a lawyer—translation: be a lawyer
—translation: does not matter   that you are a girl
—translation: I am her dream—carved out her stomach—
from her cooked hands aged from fire and bleach—her
back, a wall crumbling—her kidneys passing stones—the
weight of all her deprivation—a field of hives on her skin
—a sting piercing back.

Dialogue avec un miracle

circa. March 7, 1983

Part One

Numero Un—one day I will tell you about your sister. The first year I lost a child I cried many days and your father prayed and my mother consoled me. She had held dead babies too. And your grandmother you will love. She will spoil you, gaté-ou. She will.

Deux—the year after, I thought this was God healing me from the first. I think I must teach you to wait. To understand the way a mango tree grows. That we take for granted when they surround us, their fruit does not come for six years.

Trois—you must learn your numbers. My father removed me from school you know. He let my brothers finish but not me. And my mother did not fight. I will fight. I will fight I will fight.

Quatre—when I lost Marjorie I did not know it would be this long a wait for another. I thought something broke inside me. Your father still prayed. Everyone prayed. I fasted on the mountainside. I broke coconuts daily and drank the water. And the night came and went and I waited.

Cinq—you will meet your cousins soon. I watched my brothers' wives bear children. I must be Sarah. Did not God promise Abraham the stars?

Six—say thank you sometime when you get here. Especially to your uncle. He is the one who made you American. Now you must really learn your numbers. All I have known in this country is cleaning floors.

Sept—all the years I've waited. Today I will eat a mango
for you and I will send for my mother. You should hear
her voice. Not sad like at the airport when she put her
hands on my belly like this. Do you remember what she
said? Silly woman thought she would never see you. I
promised God this day would be holy. The day you decide
to arrive. I will kiss your little feet. And I'd like to eat
chicken again and tasso and griot. I wonder if you will
still like fish but we will fast on your birthday because
you are a gift.
Learn your numbers past seven—if
tomorrow you are born, you will remember
how many years it took to make you.

Love,
Mama
n

Dialogue avec un miracle

circa. March 7, 1983

Part Two

Words fail me now—   I have been reading   the
book of Daniel   & there is prophecy there.
        I will call you Daniel.   If you are a girl
I will call you Danielle. I wanted to name you
Colin   but your mother...   was against it.
Maybe   it can serve you as a middle name. Maybe
            one day I will tell you   about a man
who came
to Artibonite whose name I carry. I—   we have been
waiting eternity—   Tomorrow,

your mother's mother—   I spend hours fixing
words together. People wait to hear the word
of God—a waterfall   from my mouth—it is so
much easier on a pulpit.

When I see you on the other side of this sea, I will hold
you. I will tell you how we   knelt for you—how you
are the answer to our prayers. One day I will bring you
here.   Show you the Artibonite River & rice fields—how
they grow for miles—how the rain makes streams of our
village streets.

One day when you are old enough I will tell you about my
mother's hands—what they made   of my life—
how sugarcane holds sweet water   under its

hard shell—how she died in front of my eyes.

Tomorrow, I will still be away   to bury your
mother's mother.   She does not know. Keep her safe until
I get there. Keep her safe

until I get there.

Love,
Papi

American on our breath

Last I was in Port-au-Prince
We all ate avoine on the rooftop
while the daylight sung its final notes
Someone's clothes lay flat on a tin roof to dry
A muffler popped in the distance
turning the corner of broken glass road
& we talked about this Ayiti
with mangoes growing in the yard for the picking
& eggplant just ripe enough
to make a legume for the next day.
How the air brushed our skin
& this oatmeal porridge kept us warm.
A neighbor lit a fire to burn trash in a can &
every so often the breeze would carry the smell toward
us,
not enough to make us retreat but enough to be aware
there is trash & it needs burning.
I remember I stared at the flames,
thought how it lit up this little corner of the world.

Kreyol heavy on my tongue like wet earth,
English tugs war behind my teeth
& my cousin years ago, on a bumpy ride from Verrettes
called me *ti blanc* but how I needed to belong
somewhere. It was this I was holding on to. This home.
The streets now reek of tires burning
A man on camera burns an American flag & blood
smears on the street from police shooting at protestors.
I remember when Ayiti sung to me moin gin espoua

how even after being haunted by a congregation of ghosts
lost souls swallowed by the earth,
the living fight against its teeth.

Thought how hope lit up this little corner of the world
I remember, I stared at the flames.
There is trash & it needs burning
not enough to make us retreat but enough to be aware
every so often the breeze would carry the smell toward
us.
A neighbor lit a fire to burn trash in a can
& this oatmeal porridge kept us warm.
How the air brushed our skin
to make a legume for the next day,
eggplant just ripe enough.
With mangoes growing in the yard for the picking,
we talked about this Ayiti.
Turning the corner of broken glass road,
a muffler popped in the distance.
Someone's clothes lay flat on a tin roof to dry.
While the daylight sung its final notes,
we all ate avoine on the rooftop
last I was in Port-au-Prince.

My father says *it may be long*
before we go again
That it is too dangerous to leave
with American on our breath
& I think then, where
where exactly is home?

Colin (masculine)
co·lin | KAHL-in

Meaning
1: a boy (a name for a boy)

2: whelp (or otherwise a puppy)

3: of a triumphant people; people's victory

Usage in a sentence
The father gave his first name Colin as a middle name to his daughter. In that way, she is a Junior. Perhaps he wanted a boy. Perhaps she is his victory.

The Father begets the Daughter

All my life I watched you, papi
make your flock fly on Sunday.
When I was a child, it was easy
to watch in awe, the lightning of the sermon,
how it hovered over my head to make me miracle
how the sound of my voice drowned.

Between languages my tongue drowned
praising the Father but never praising my papi
out loud. It took eight years to make me miracle
in the womb of my mother & Sunday
became the only day a sermon
made conversation between us easy

To be taken to the park would have been easy,
pushed by you on a swing instead of drowned
in listening from the pew for your sermon,
the way I searched for you in the bleachers, papi.
I wondered while church met on Sunday
what could make the girl in me more miracle

than the son you never had. Miracle
sounds so much smaller in a heart uneasy
in secrets. How do I testify on Sunday
without ever feeling drowned?
I learned to speak your language, papi
a poem bred from a sermon

On the Mount called Vernon was the sermon

you took hours to write—a miracle
light under your office door kept you papi
awake & away & it was never easy
to share your laugh, to drown
in the congregation on Sunday.

How I know you love me the way you love Sunday
but I am still the child waiting for the sermon
to come home to, jump out from a corner—drowned
in the joy of making a game of miracles
instead of being one. Might have been easy—
more (or less) to have a Pastor for a papi.

But the road to Sunday is paved with miracles
missing sermons that never take it easy,
sacrificed moments drowned in this ache for my papi.

The Sermon

The light shone and the land rose from a thought
in my mind and a word from my mouth
And yet I needed no mouth to speak it,
nor lips to make syllables sound out
I spoke and the birds spread their
wings along the surface of the air
The sparrows had my eye though my vision was
everywhere present in a blade of grass,
the curve of a cloud, the rugged side of mountains
the smooth bottom of a baby's backside,
I am Life in John 11:25
I am life's bread in John 6. Life feeds on my existence,
my everlasting presence and I am present, here and now
effervescent and luminescent. I threw balls of fire
in the sky and made the earth move
to shape the moon's crescent
laced in the night like a smile
and I was content with what I
made. In Luke 1:78 I am the Dayspring, the rising
sun pushing darkness back against the horizon
I am Judah's lion, the only begotten son,
yet I and the Father are
one and we and the Spirit are three
I am the Trinity
Jehovah Nissi, Jirai,
Rapha, Shammah, Raah,
Tsidkenu, Mehodishkem, Shalom,
Elohim, El Shaddai, Adonai
Which only means I provide, shepherd, heal, sanctify.
I am forever and beyond. I am beyond forever.
In the beginning I was the beginning
I was the beginning's beginning and I am before the
beginning's beginning began
I am the great I AM

I am God
And I chose YOU
To love without condition, without reservation,
To be a royal priesthood and holy nation
Took my time with your creation
molded wonderfully, fearfully,
masterfully, awesomely from the earth in my hand
Every wrinkle, every mark, every bone, every strand
If only you could understand who I am
Then perhaps you would wonder less where
I Am, when
I Am, if
I Am
And the love that embodies me would embody you
If you would accept the simple truth that
I AM
GOD

The Poem

Poem be like hello,
how are you?
Poem be like be
creative with your answer.
I'm fine just won't do.
Poem be like I know
the real you, crouching
in the corner
of your mind.
I know where you hide
& go seek
Poem be like,
did you find
what you were looking for?
Sits in the living room
like guests do. Strips
the couch of its
plastic & lounges
for a while. Poem be
like who needs a couch?
This rug is nice. Poem
be like we need some color
on the walls. Poem be
writing on the wall
like love letters from God.
Poem be like remember
where you came from.
Poem be like remember
where I came from.
Poem be like you
the messenger. I'm just here
to make sure you speak.
Make sure you write
when you weep—

when you smile—
when you snarl—
when you pray.
Poem be conversing
all day in verses
like *can we talk for a minute*
or two
or one thousand
or infinity.
Poem don't leave
until poem does
what poem do. Poem be re
visiting your vision
like relatives come
to reminiscence.
Poem be family.
Poem be love.
Poem be memory.
Poem be verbs conjugating
to their own music.
Poem be words
for the speechless.
be like 3 am is
when we work out.
Poem be counting
syllables like push-ups
& haikus be part
of the same training.
Poem be like
make the church
say amen. This right
here is hallelujah language.
Poem be like
I see you.
I see you
when you don't

see yourself.
Poem be like write,
write
long enough
& you will.

Danielle (feminine)

dan·ielle | dan-YEL

Meaning

1: girl's name derived from French

2: female modification of the name Daniel

2: meaning 'God is my judge' in Hebrew

Usage in a sentence

If it all goes right with a name like Danielle, even lions cannot devour her. Instead one day she may be loved by one.

Call me Adjoa

Ashanti Twi for
      born on Monday

I'm from Immigrant mother
      finding soil to name her child
            citizen.Call me American dream
come to roost
      to wreck tables
          & sit down
anyway

I am from dried breast milk
      language for grandmothers
          dying from even our sons
          do not protect us from their fathers
from strong backs, weak hearts
      & summer heat in winter
          conceived in a language
I am not sure now was love
      but necessary
Call me a lesson learning
to unlearn wounds

I am from big belly
    & first
        & only

I'm from calabashes empty
      for water, a womb filled

              an outcry of motherhood
call me miracle

from b-r-e-a-k   &   s-i-l-e-n-c-e
mouthing syllables together

I am from preacher blood
        from holy men who say
              women are supposed to
from mask I mastered
        for religion
              Call me an unmasking for God

Call me sermon
        Call me poem,
              rebirth of a word
                    burned to my tongue

Call me a birthing
        A shell breaking
              Say my name in Hebrew
              God is my judge
The rest is none
        of anyone's business

less I make it known

What is it they say?

What's in the dark
        eventually comes to light?

Call me a reckoning
a new day
a 24 hour sit-in
protest in this here sun

Response to *I remember you. You're his ex-girlfriend.*

Just so you know,
I have since become
the sun. I carry the universe
in my imagination. The stars
have since become my toys. I play
hopscotch on constellations & laugh
with Andromeda about monsters loosed
to slay us. The ocean cannot hold
me. I used it
to wash him away.
You see,
I am not just his
Ex-girl-
friend. I am his lost
love. The letter inside the bottle.
I have since broken
the glass. His heart,
left there to bleed—
I am not sorry.
What you did not see
was the car speeding toward red
light & screeching brakes
to terrorize me, my smile crumbling
like wet sand from my fingers,
how slow time came to
rescue me, how my heart can
hold torment & love. I cannot explain.
I have since found the diamonds
I'd misplaced, put them back

in my mouth. I am found,
like a seashell to its song
You see, I am more.
I have since remembered my self.

That thing on my head

When my hair was relaxed the only
two questions asked were:
Is it real? And what do you use?
Now that I've transitioned from
straight hair to my natural self
it's like people have hypertension
share all sorts of comments
and questions like: How long does that take you?
and then there is my pet peeve: *Can I touch it?*
as if I'm some type of of exotic pet. Go find a poodle.

Or comments like: *You know Easter Sunday is coming up.*
What are you going to do with THAT?
This is usually accompanied by a look of concern
Or why didn't you comb your hair today?...Oh, it's combed?
But you can't run the comb through?...Oh, you can?
But how do you get it this soft?...Wait, it's soft?
All of these are usually accompanied by a look of
confusion
And the list goes on like:

> * *Are you ever going to straighten THAT?*
> * *I mean you're going to straighten THAT for your*
>   *wedding right?*
> * *I mean, c'mon, how do you expect to get a man? A*
>   *job?*
> * *You don't think you look like an old lady?*

Whoa.
[Speechless with raised eyebrows.]

> * *Did you stick your finger in an electrical socket this*
>   *morning?*

No. But I know WHO
I can stick in an electrical socket!

* Are you Jamaican?

[Again. Speechless.]
They're two strand twists,
not locs & then not all
Jamaicans have locs...?

* So why don't you just get locs?!

I see this is a pointless conversation

Makes me want to have discussions
on the effects of colonialism on the mind
the brainwashing of the media
the overwhelming abundance of images showing
Black women with long flowing hair
when we really know the truth
when we know even with a relaxer,
our hair blows in the wind only
on the day we leave the salon and then it's all hope.

Makes me want to have arguments
like if a man only wants me
because I have straight hair
maybe he shouldn't have me at all

& if a job won't hire me
maybe I need to hire myself

& if you can't handle
looking at my hair on Easter Sunday
maybe you should question why it is you go to church

Besides the fact that *this thing* on my head
you refer to as *THAT*
is just the way it grows.

Salty Monkey (2005)

That's the problem with America
    All these Black people
Need to go back
    To Africa
        Damn monkeys
Need to get rid of them
    Start all over
Then America
    Will be fine

        says white man sitting in the middle
of the city bus
        talking to himself
          five of us Black folk in the
back

        ears perched on his words

What did he say?
    What the—

        Black lips twist & hurl
        insults like empty casings

Can't even talk right
    All those damn holes
In your mouth
    In your clothes
        White man laughs
        through missing teeth
        his long white beard
        lusterless & flapping
        on his chin
Makak salé!

        I think in my mind.
        It sounds good in Kreyol—

doesn't taste right on my tongue
in English—salty monkey.

Young Black girl reading her book
looks up—opens her mouth
catches my eyes—
whatever she is about to say
sounds like

Makak salé!

out loud
but we're both quiet
idioms vexed in our eyes

for every Black Woman who has been called Angry

I've been trying not to be an angry Black woman/ make
sure I smile a little in public/Seems like the
understanding is that our facial expressions/do not lend
to other emotions
that the fear is we stay ready/to start a commotion
just because   like there are no reasons to be

Black,
a woman
& angry at the same time

so don't you know on most days/I turn/my smile into a
protest
but the rest is a crooked upwards battle/I've been trying
to rise like Maya's dust/every time there's some bitter
twisted lies,
been trying to be Black girl magic/without a spell
to conjure over this hurt/this pain/this rolled up
thunder pressed between my ears/I been trying to
sew invisibility cloaks to drape
around my children
for protection,
only to find out/they invisible already/
without protection—been trying
to tell my daughters/to not be angry/that sass
might get you
sassed/that kissing the pavement/ain't better
than going home.
They will say you had too much attitude—

refuse to see your smile
pressing through from behind your teeth—the world
on your shoulders
like the mule you are—they will wonder how
you made it anyhow—how somehow
they haven't killed you yet—
being angry and all

...& ain't that the point—that Harriet Tubman
had to be an angry Black woman—that Sojourner Truth
had to be an angry Black woman—that Assata Shakur
had to be an angry Black woman—that Fannie Lou
Hamer had to be an angry Black woman—that Rosa
Parks
had to be an angry Black womam—that Shirley Chisolm
had to be an angry Black woman—that Ida B. Wells
had to be an angry Black woman—that Coretta Scott King
had to be an angry Black woman—that Betty Shabazz
had to be an angry Black woman

...& ain't that the point—
that I have every right
to be angry/Angry about
our trees cut down & the roots left there
naked in the sun/about history being his
story/one too many times/
about corrections
to my language
when my tongue
was already cut out/about
gentrification/about

discrimination/about
appropriation of my culture/about bullets
spraying like a carnival
game on victims with no
weapons/about being called
everything but my name—
mammy—jezebel—ratchet—bitch
about the prison industrial
complex/about this reflection someone
put in the mirror that ain't my
own—I have every right
to break the glass.
This anger ain't yours
to police/ain't yours
to cage up like a bird
ain't yours
is the point.

I've been trying not to be an angry Black woman—
truth is
I ain't trying no more
& you going to be glad one day
I said you going to be glad one day
I was angry enough
to change the world.

Arkansas

She stands in front of me in line,
petite enough to fit in one of her 3 suitcases,
shuffling feet & coffee in her hand
Tries to get her ticket out
Coffee about to spill & I offer to hold the coffee
She smiles. Says *thank you.*
I nod & wonder where's she's headed
with all that stuff. On the bus
She offers the seat next to her
No more window seats. Coffee made us
familiar enough & I sit. Say *thank you.*

She examines her ticket to Arkansas
It unfolds over her lap & we laugh about how long
her ticket is—how long she has to ride the bus
Her smile dwindles. She shows me a photo of her son
Her eyes focus on me & she says
I don't know why I'm telling you this
but I just left my abusive husband
& I need to get my son back.

We have two & a half hours to New York City
I let her fill all the time she needs with her story—her
life,
her isolation from the world—wakeful nights—court dates
—

love—heartbreak—renewal—escape—hollowness—hell
& her son, lost from her arms & her desperation
to get him away—out out of Canada
out from his father's custody—out from hell out

She doesn't know how or even if she can
but she will.

All I have is a poem & a belief in meeting people
on purpose. All I have is a poem I let her keep.
The one I hadn't let anyone read
because I only wrote it for me

She reads. Tears in our eyes
seeing all the reasons I'm not with him
all the reasons she left him
& how we used to love

Us, two women
strangers who know each other
in stories meant for greyhound buses

Half-spent Bus Ride

she's half spent like her two way bus fare
with a baby on her arm
& one in her womb
wearing weary in her eyes
& steel cheeks that make me wonder
how often they rise into a smile.

she looks like
thinking plagues her mind,
the chase of life
crumbles everything she touches.
she's sick of being alive & not
living.

today is just another day
dragging slow like the fatigue
creeping through her pregnant
body. she's carrying
life. she's carrying
life. she's carrying life
half spent; half alive

I watch her from my seat,
inside me a painful
memory of a memory of wanting babies
awakes from the sleep I tucked it away in.

she reminds me of lost dreams
& little girls who considered living
before death could tease.

I watch her from my seat
so much noise around me
but inside I hear
only my thoughts croon
for the rest of the bus ride.

On the Corner of Washington & Swan

She look like she used to
sing with jazz musicians
Bessie Smith singing
Nobody knows you when you down and out
she holds her brow steady
shoulders back like a dancer
dancing in her mind
to songs of struggle and life
ready to ask she inhales to prep
for the question, holds her breath
for the answer and exhales
to keep from dying. She's met
so much silence. All she hears
is her own voice
bouncing off the noise that surrounds her,
surround sound silencing her

She stands on the corner of Washington and Swan
on the corner right behind
the capital building where government
don't see her; where vendors sell
hot dogs and relish and
the hot sun reminds her what hell is
she's been standing like homelessness
never breaks her spirit
she's been waiting for change
truth is she's been asking for spare change
so she could have change to spare
truth is she was waiting for change
back when everybody in her hood

wanted to be something
realized more people wanted them
to be nothing; they didn't know
how to Be
something and the ones that did
weren't sharing the wealth,
no knowledge to spare like these people
who only got folded
twenty dollar bills in their pockets
that aren't for giving,
people who left her hood
went on living.
she was waiting for change
back when she still felt like change could
change into dollar sense
and sense into what society calls success
all she has now is her sense with no cents

she's standing there
on the corner of Washington and Swan
where her clock is
ticking to the sound of heels
clacking the sidewalk fresh suit tails
wagging in the breeze. They rock
the slacks with sneakers on their lunch breaks
to Dunkin Donuts for their ice coffees
pass by her to the vendors to buy
hot dogs, french fries and icees
but it seems nobody sees what her eyes see
unless it's directly related to their own reality

She's stands there
on the corner of Washington and Swan

where the buses stop
where people carrying bus fare
wish they could share what they don't have
they know what lessness is
so close to it they could taste it
as she swallows
the gratefulness in them that they're
not in her shoes. She's been asking for
monetary assistance loose unchanging change
changing nothing except
the fact that she might eat today.
her melodic voice continues
she's singing the blues
      she's singing the blues
           she's singing the blues
to the jazz of car horns, jingling keys,
the drum of her heartbeat and
one last chord
that keeps her unashamed to survive.

Loved by a Lion

A bird pooped on me
on the way here & I heard
your voice in my head
loud, say *motherfucker*
& I said *yeah, exactly. This is poop*
I hate birds but you
know that already & now
that I'm standing here,
palm flat on the surface of this
door, I don't want to go inside
Burn the body you said
Keep my ashes you said
so I brought that duffel bag
you know the one
packed all your hats—all seventeen
& your Lion's jersey
& suddenly I feel
like the Lions,
losing all the time
because I've lost you & I packed
all the wrong things—
these shoes & pants don't matter.
I whisper to the door *I'll be back*
leave the weight on the floor.
You need all your cameras
so I go get them—all 9 of them.
I use the rest of the ink
in the printer for all the pictures
you've taken of me

& when I come back, I look
for a handle where there is none
so I push,
see the weight of you on the table,
stand with my back against the door
shut behind me
like I'm posing for a picture
but you do not move.
I say out loud *I brought all your cameras.*
They are here
in these bags. Can you see
me like you always have?
I say *mwen pa kapab* & I wish
I taught you more Kreyol
but I know no language for this
so I pull my feet up & forward
one by one to get close.
Run my hand along the side of your body
from your ankle to the freckles on your cheek.
I hear you say *you still don't like my feet*
& I ask how you do that
Speak from the dead that is/*You know*
I don't like feet/In general
This ain't about yours
I'm sorry about getting snippy
There are worse things than feet
dry skin flaking off the heels.
You should have drunk more water love.

I run my fingers through your beard
detangle the strands
caress the silver

lift your head gently
gather up your locs
interlock them as a braid
wrap the braid around itself
unloose it all
let your hair hang
off the side of the table
run my fingers
through the coarseness
feel it tickle my skin a little
lift a handful to my nose
breathe you in
wanting to smell a remnant
of Egyptian musk. I feel
tears on my face
eyes shut, water falling.
Wipe my face with your hair
I am Mary Magdalene
& you loved me. You were
nothing my parents expected
my first major act of defiance
I feel emptied of your divinity.
I wonder if you ever knew
you were divine. I should have told you.
I smooth my hand across your forehead,
coax your edges
to lay
but they are as rebellious
as we are & I pull
all the pictures out
lay them one by one on your body,
say *this is how you loved me*

This is how you loved me
This is how you loved me
Rub your belly like a Buddha &
lay another picture
This is how you loved me
This is how I smiled with you
This is how I laughed with you
This is what my beauty looks like in your lens
& when you are covered
in photographs I know
they will think me strange.
I will say *burn it all*
That's all the fire we had between us.
That's what I want to keep
how you loved me
how you loved
& I'll be wearing
this Lion's jersey.

On the Pulse of Morning

January 20, 2017

Today, I looked at the sky. I heard the call of the
crows
black winged & flying on a warm January afternoon.
They give me pause when I leave work. I become
keenly aware of my pulse. When my heart stops
I believe there will be a bird pecking at its last beat.

Ever since seventeen,
I have never known peace at the sight of beaks
flocks flocking together; organizing
like they are also in protest
like they will march across a DC sky
tonight to prepare for tomorrow

If too close this fear forces
flinch in my eye
well of tears,
clench of my fists
swift movement of my feet in safety's direction
but today, the crows cawed my name

made me turn my face to look up

welcome their terror as an ally, an omen of change

I should have cried

trembled like a child at winter air's mercy

but today I breathed—

today, the crows came by the hundreds

like ancestors come to fill me with their pulsing histories

like a meeting of souls come to teach

their wings weep across my heart like a

widow in mourning

numbed by an open casket but I know this

ride home ain't no regular home going

I will grieve for what is lost;

sing a new song of

freedom to the caw of crows

gathering to send messages from

the other side. I will be walking with ghosts

with fists in the air.

I should have been afraid

but today I felt nothing less than my pulse

I am alive &

history needs me.

Thank you to the editors and publications who accepted earlier
versions of these poems:
"That thing on my head" [Anthology forthcoming]
"Soutien" [Anthology forthcoming]
"Broke just like that" *Ink & Nebula*

I am indebted to the wonderful feedback of Cap City Slam, Cave
Canem, VONA fellows and faculty in the last year. Many thanks to
Patricia Smith, Willie Perdomo, Dawn Lundy-Martin, Cornelius Eady,
Raymond Antrobus, Cameron Awkward-Rich, Taylor Johnson, Justin
Phillip Reed, April Freely, Jasmine Elizabeth Smith, El Williams,
Shay Lawz, Raina Leon, Alan Chazaro, Chavonn Shen, Jenise Miller,
Jade Yeung, Gemelle John, Soleil David, Lena Blackmon, Olivia
Mckee, Amani Olugbala, Laura Evelyn for your generous insight on
my work.

Shout out to Chelsea Celestain, Dante Micheaux, Ashunda Norris,
Jennifer Falu, Mahogany L. Browne, Camonghne Felix, Toi Dericotte,
Elizabeth Acevedo, Ibi Zoboi, Abiodun Ayewole for sharing
encouraging words, time and memorable affirming moments.

Many, many thank yous to Black Theater Troupe of Upstate New
York, The New York State Writers Institute, The Arts Center of the
Capital Region, Capital Rep Theater, Sandglass Theater, The
Sanctuary for Independent Media, Albany Social Justice Center,

Creative Action Unlimited, The New York State Museum, Children at the Well, Troy Kitchen and the many folks who have provided space for me to write, teach and perform. You make the idea of being a full-time poet possible.

Poetic Vibe family, I love you! It's an honor to curate this open mic and to be part of this community. Power Breakfast (Jessica Wayde, Karyn Dyer, Jamel Mosely, Roberta Singleton) you have kept me motivated and inspired. I push because we push together.

Thank you to the homies near and far, Elizabeth King, Mairlyne Whilby, Rachelle Anilus, Tarishi Shuler, Peter Seaton, Daniel Summerhill, Chelle Pean, Elizabeth K. Gordon, Terry St. Jean, Keion Hennessey and so many more I don't have enough page space to thank for checking up on me, rooting me on, collaborating and most of all showing up when I needed you most.

Gwendolyn Hayles, thank you for your daughter being a part of the cover.

To my parents, I love you & I do not take lightly the investment of time, energy, sacrifice and love that has gone into raising me to this person I am. Thank you.

To my love, Robert Cooper, thank you for all the photos for this book and beyond but above all that, thank you for being my best friend. It is beautiful to be loved by a lion.

Most of all thank you to the Most High for this gift called poetry.

About the Author

D. Colin, author of *Dreaming in Kreyol,* is a first generation Haitian American poet currently residing in Troy, NY. Her poem "Broke just like that" appears in Ink & Nebula. Her work, *Simone,* a hybrid between poetry and theater, debuted this year at Capital Rep Theater and tells the story of a Haitian immigrant earthquake survivor fighting against the threat of deportation. She has performed on national platforms and featured internationally in Toronto and the UK. Her weekly open mic, Poetic Vibe, was voted Best Open Mic in the Capital Region in 2018 and she was named one of New York Capital Region's 2019 Creatives under 40 in *The Collaborative*. Holding a Bachelors in English and a Masters in Africana Studies, she is also a fellow of Cave Canem, VONA and the New York State Writers Institute. To learn more visit www.dcolin.com.

CPSIA information can be obtained
at www.ICGtesting.com
Printed in the USA
FFHW012158090719
53533559-59186FF

LWV LEAGUE OF WOMEN VOTERS®
OF SARATOGA COUNTY

Presents~

Breakfast with Shirley Chisholm
(portrayed by Kim Wafer)
Directed by Lezlie Dana
The Inn at Saratoga
July 18, 2020, 9am

"Service is the rent we pay for room
on this earth."

Kim Wafer has had the pleasure of working with a number of theater groups in the Capital Region. Some of her favorite roles have been Ruth (Raisin in the Sun), Harriet Tubman, Sojourner Truth, Vivian Baptiste (Lesson Before Dying), Mrs. Birling (Inspector Calls), and Della (Greenwood: A Dream Destroyed) to name a few. She is honored and delighted to portray the powerful Shirley Chisholm: the first black woman to be elected to the US Congress and first African American woman to run for the Presidential Candidacy of the US.

SHIRLEY CHISHOLM (1924 - 2005)

"Tremendous amounts of talent are lost to our society just because that talent wears a skirt." Shirley Chisholm made history as the first African-American woman elected to Congress (1968). Through seven consecutive terms in Congress, she was a passionate advocate for minority rights and urban needs. She staffed her Congressional office entirely with women, half of whom were African-American. Her campaign slogan was "Unbought and Unbossed."

Chisolm began her career in early childhood education, running a day care center and after retiring from Congress went back to teaching- this time at Mount Holyoke College. When she retired from Congress she remarked, *"When I ran for the Congress, when I ran for president, I met more discrimination as a woman than for being black. Men are men."*

The League of Women Voters is a nonpartisan organization that encourages informed and active participation in government. We never support candidates or political parties.

We are the League of Women Voters of Saratoga County, a local chapter of the League of Women Voters of New York State and the national League of Women Voters.

The League of Women Voters encourages informed and active participation in government, works to increase understanding of major public policy issues, and influences public policy through education and advocacy.

League of Women Voters of Saratoga County
PO Box 1029
Saratoga Springs, NY 12866
Email to president@lwvsaratoga.org
www.lwvsaratoga.org
www.facebook.com/lwvsaratoga
Twitter @LWV_SC
Instagram @lwvsaratoga